Table of Contents

Meet Pat Cummings

Pat Cummings and her sister Linda

Pat Cummings has been drawing ever since she was a little girl. Her family moved a lot because her father was in the army. "I found if I joined the art club or helped make posters for other clubs it was a way to make new friends," Pat Cummings says.

The author with some of her family

Artie

Pat

Pat Cummings often writes stories about her family and her own childhood. *Clean Your Room, Harvey Moon!* is about her brother Artie and the funny things he did.

Pat Cummings with her cat, Cash

CLEAN

HOUGHTON MIFFLIN COMPANY
BOSTON
ATLANTA   DALLAS   GENEVA, ILLINOIS   PALO ALTO   PRINCETON

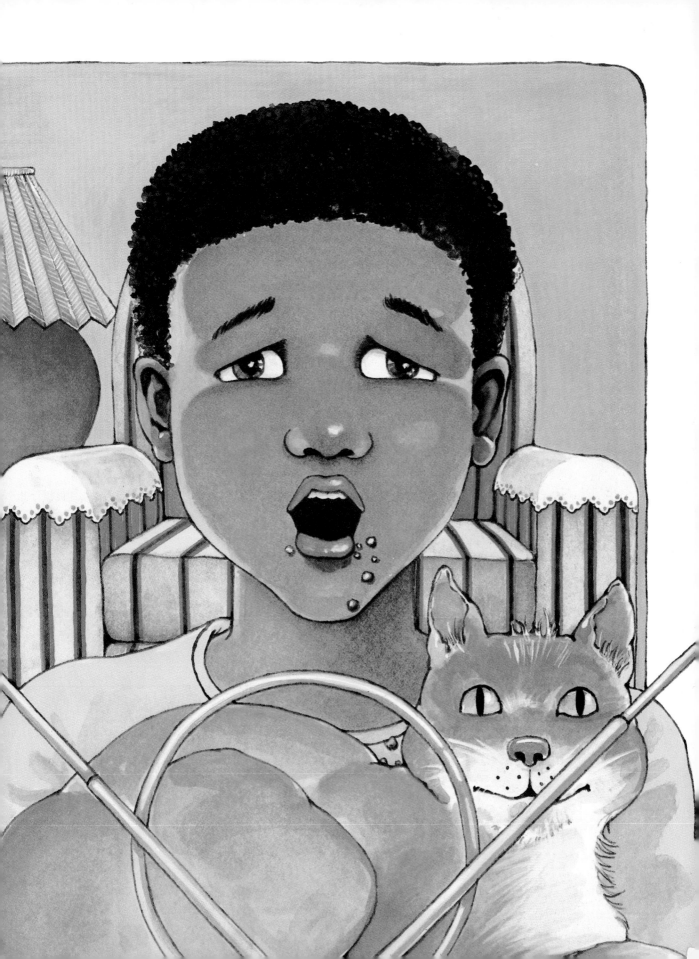

"Not nowwww . . . " moaned Harvey,
Red in the face.
"I'll miss 'Rotten Ed'
And 'Invaders from Space'!"
"Right this second!" she ordered,
And gave him the broom.
Harvey marched angrily
Up to his room.

It really didn't seem
Messy at all.
First he'd throw his dirty clothes
Out in the hall.
Under the bed was
An ice cream-smeared shirt,
Jeans that had what Mom called
"Ground-in dirt. . . ."

Two towels and swim trunks
That seemed to be wet,
Three socks he sniffed
And found weren't dirty yet.
Under the dresser was a lump
Warm and gray,
That he didn't recognize
So he put it away.

The floor of the closet had clumps
Hard and dirty
Of T-shirts and sweatshirts. . . .
IT WAS TEN-THIRTY!
Harvey panicked then thought,
"I should be through soon,
I'll eat lunch while I watch
'Creature Zero' at noon."

Grabbing marbles and crayons and
Flat bottle caps,
Two of his own special
Lightning bug traps,
The softball he couldn't find
Last Saturday,
One toothbrush, one helmet . . .
He put them away.

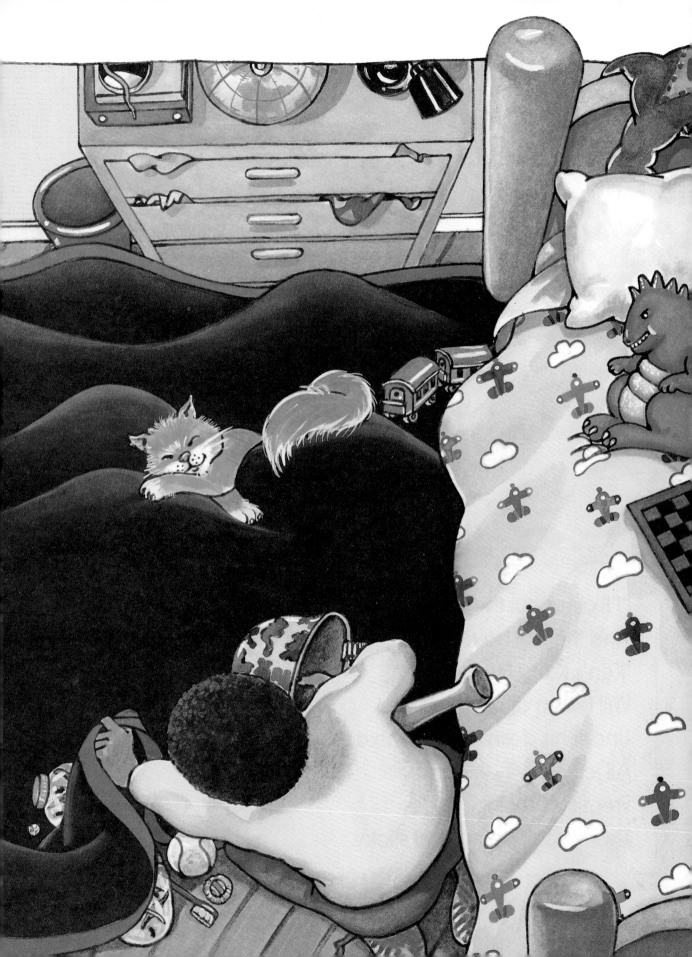

"I'll clear out these toys
And then I'll be done,
'Ken's Kung Fu Korner'
Will be on at one. . . ."
Under his desk were some comics
All icky
From something inside
That was dripping and sticky.

21

He found library books
He'd forgotten he had,
His skates from Aunt Sarah,
His bow tie from dad,
He found a caboose
That was missing its train,
A whistle, paintbrushes,
A map of the brain.

23

He found sneakers and card games
Up under the bed,
Goggles, flippers, and a grasshopper
. . . dead,
A long-lost cookie
All fuzzy and gray,
Plastic cars, boats, and planes,
And he put them away.

Just then Harvey happened
To notice the clock.
"IT'S ALMOST TWO!!" Harvey shouted.
He went into shock.
"I missed 'Caveman Capers'
On channel nine. . . .
I'm starving! I'm tired!
This room looks fine!"

He put up his bathrobe,
His bat, and football,
With a few other things
Then ran down the hall,
Shouting, "Mom, I'm finished!"
Harvey put back the broom.
His mother stepped cautiously
Into his room.

"I'm really amazed," his mom said.
Harvey beamed.
He could watch TV now. He was through,
So it seemed.
"I fixed you some lunch," she said.
"When you are done,
You and I will get started
On lump number one!"

THE END?

Kids' Work

Costa Rica

Carrying milk to the house

33

China

Working in a field

Shoveling snow

United States

Painting house shutters

United States

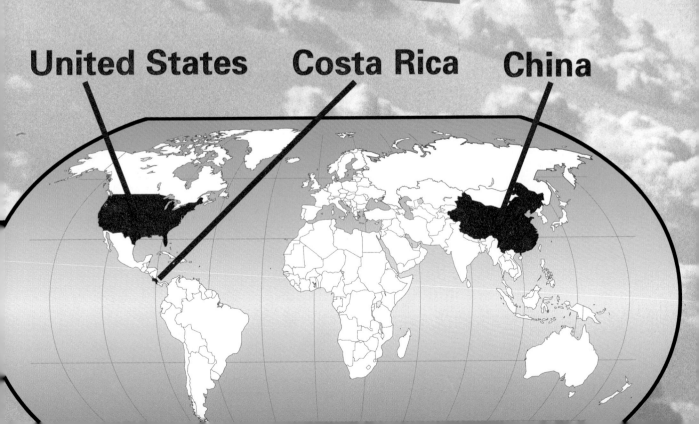

United States   Costa Rica   China

LOOK CLOSELY

Look closely at the picture of this room. Can you find the crayons? Can you find the socks? What else do you see?

Pick Up Your Room *by Mary Ann Hoberman*

Pick up your room, my mother says
    (She says it every day);
My room's too heavy to pick up
    (That's what I always say).

It's time to take a bath, she says
    (She looks me in the eye);
Where shall I take it to? I ask
    (That's always my reply).

Drink up your milk, she says to me,
    Don't bubble like a clown;
Of course she knows I'll answer that
    I'd rather drink it down.

And when she says at eight o'clock,
    You must go right to bed,
We both repeat my answer:
    Why not go left instead?

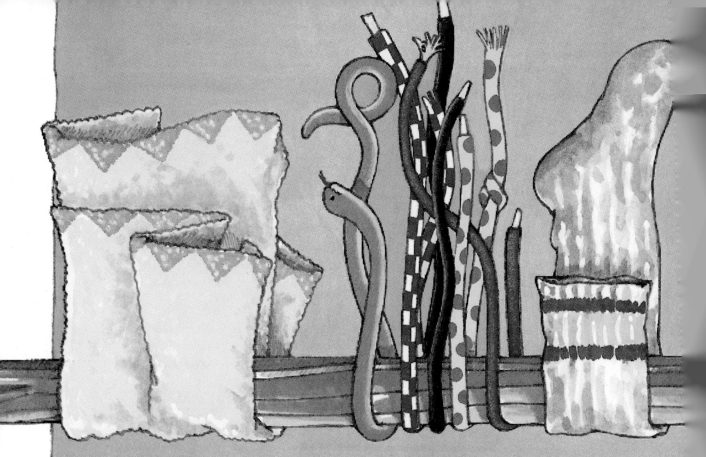

by Pat Cummings

YOUR ROOM, HARVEY MOON!

Acknowledgments

Grateful acknowledgment is made for use of the following material:

Text

2 *Clean Your Room, Harvey Moon!*, written and illustrated by Pat Cummings. Copyright © 1991 by Pat Cummings. Reprinted by permission of Macmillan Books for Young Readers, Simon & Schuster Children's Publishing Division. **36** "Look Closely," from March 1992 *Sesame Street Magazine*. Copyright © 1992 by Children's Television Workshop. Reprinted by permission. **38** "Pick Up Your Room," from *Fathers, Mothers, Sisters, Brothers,* by Mary Ann Hoberman, illustrated by Marylin Hafner. Text copyright © 1991 by Mary Ann Hoberman. Reprinted by permission of Little, Brown and Company.

Illustrations

33 Christine Czernota (globe).

Photography

i Tony Scarpetta. **ii–iii** Courtesy Pat Cummings; Tony Scarpetta (background). **33** © Rose Welch. **33–35** © David Muscroft/Tony Stone Images (background). **34** © Catherine Ursillo/Photo Researchers (t); © Cathlyn Melloan/Tony Stone Images, Inc. (b). **35** © David Young Wolff/Tony Stone Images, Inc. (r). **36–37** Illustration © Joan Steiner, photo by Jeff Heiges. **38** Tony Scarpetta.

Houghton Mifflin Edition, 1996
Copyright © 1996 by Houghton Mifflin Company. All rights reserved.

Printed in the U.S.A.

ISBN 0-395-73169-0

56789-B-98 97 96 95

For Kali

On Saturday morning at ten to nine
Harvey Moon was eating toast,
Waiting for the cartoon show
That he enjoyed the most.

With only minutes left to go,
He heard the voice of DOOM.
"Today, young man," his mother said,
"Is the day you clean your room!"